THE SCIENCE OF ANIMAL MOVEMENT

How Fish Swim

BY EMMA HUDDLESTON

CONTENT CONSULTANT
DAVID HU, PHD
PROFESSOR
MECHANICAL ENGINEERING
GEORGIA TECH

Kids Core
An Imprint of Abdo Publishing
abdobooks.com

abdobooks.com

Published by Abdo Publishing, a division of ABDO, PO Box 398166, Minneapolis, Minnesota 55439. Copyright © 2021 by Abdo Consulting Group, Inc. International copyrights reserved in all countries. No part of this book may be reproduced in any form without written permission from the publisher. Kids Core™ is a trademark and logo of Abdo Publishing.

Printed in the United States of America, North Mankato, Minnesota
022020
092020

Cover Photo: Shutterstock Images
Interior Photos: RLS Photo/Shutterstock Images, 4–5; Rich Carey/Shutterstock Images, 7, 22–23; Kjersti Joergensen/Shutterstock Images, 8; iStockphoto, 10–11, 20 (top), 20 (bottom); Dave Alan/iStockphoto, 13; Menno Schaefer/Shutterstock Images, 14; Istomina Olena/Shutterstock Images, 16–17; Aksenova Natalya/Shutterstock Images, 19 (top); Zacarias Pereira da Mata/Shutterstock Images, 19 (bottom); Ramon Carretero/Shutterstock Images, 24; Shutterstock Images, 26; Picture Partners/Shutterstock Images, 28; Eric Isselee/Shutterstock Images, 29 (top); Gerald Robert Fischer/Shutterstock Images, 29 (bottom)

Editor: Marie Pearson
Series Designer: Ryan Gale

Library of Congress Control Number: 2019954079

Publisher's Cataloging-in-Publication Data

Names: Huddleston, Emma, author.
Title: How fish swim / by Emma Huddleston
Description: Minneapolis, Minnesota : Abdo Publishing, 2021 | Series: The science of animal movement | Includes online resources and index.
Identifiers: ISBN 9781532192951 (lib. bdg.) | ISBN 9781644944349 (pbk.) | ISBN 9781098210854 (ebook)
Subjects: LCSH: Children's questions and answers--Juvenile literature. | Fishes--Swimming--Juvenile literature. | Science--Examinations, questions, etc--Juvenile literature. | Habits and behavior--Juvenile literature.
Classification: DDC 500--dc23

CONTENTS

CHAPTER 1
Moving through Water 4

CHAPTER 2
Resistance 10

CHAPTER 3
Body Shape 16

CHAPTER 4
Buoyancy 22

Movement Diagram 28
Glossary 30
Online Resources 31
Learn More 31
Index 32
About the Author 32

Fish that live in coral reefs, including the queen angelfish, need to be able to make tight turns.

CHAPTER 1

Moving through Water

A queen angelfish swims near shore in the western Atlantic Ocean. Its bright yellow tail fin beats back and forth. The fish's thin body fits between cracks in rocks. It changes direction often to avoid coral. Its small body fins help it stop and turn.

Bodies and Fins

Most fish have smooth bodies, fins, and tails. Yet each species is a different size, shape, and color. Fish's bodies **adapt** to where they live in order to survive.

More than 85 percent of fish swim by wriggling their bodies and tails. They use their fins to steer. Some fish, such as eels, move their bodies in many curves. The curves ripple down

Swimming Speed

The fastest fish swim with their tails. Strong, quick beats push their bodies through the water. Fish that swim with their body fins are slower. Body fins help fish move around objects.

their bodies. Other fish, such as trout, move their bodies less.

Tuna swim through the ocean. They can swim in bursts faster than 40 miles per hour (64 km/h).

The way rays move their fins in the water can resemble a bird slowly flapping its wings.

Another way fish swim is by flapping their fins. This type of swimming is important for fish on the seafloor. They have to move around objects. This kind of fish usually has a wide tail and a pair of fins on its sides. Others have **horizontal** wing-like fins. Rays are one example. But no matter a fish's shape, science affects how it swims.

Explore Online

Visit the website below. Did you learn any new information about how fish swim that wasn't in Chapter One?

How Do Fish . . . Swim?

abdocorelibrary.com/how-fish-swim

Moving water pushes against plants as well as swimming fish.

Resistance

When a fish swims, it faces resistance from the water. Resistance is a force that pushes against movement. Resistance is also called drag. A fish has to push against the water to move.

Water **particles** are packed closely together. This means that water is dense. Bodies moving through water face more drag than if they moved through air. Drag could be as much as 800 times higher underwater than in air.

Necessary Resistance

A fish usually has a **dorsal fin**. This fin runs along a fish's back. Dorsal fins use resistance to help fish balance. If a fish starts to tilt, water pushes against the fin. Sharks need dorsal fins to swim straight and keep from rolling over. Dorsal fins can also help fish steer.

It is harder for fish to swim against fast-flowing water than water moving slowly because there is more drag.

Thrust

To overcome drag, fish need to create thrust. Thrust is a force that pushes fish forward. Fish use their strong muscles to create thrust. They move their tails, bodies, and fins. They push against the water like feet push against the ground.

A salmon's powerful tail can push it through fast-flowing water.

To start moving, a fish's thrust must be stronger than the drag. Fish that swim with their tail fins create a lot of thrust. Fish that mainly use their body fins create less thrust.

Primary Source

Researcher Dominique Roche explains how a fish's swimming ability matches where it lives:

> [Some fish], such as pufferfish, are not so well equipped to handle the challenges of living in high flow environments, and prefer the peace and calm of sheltered lagoons.

Source: Dominique Roche. "Why Some Fish Can't Go with the Flow." *Phys.org*, 7 Mar. 2014, phys.org. Accessed 25 Oct. 2019.

Comparing Texts

Think about the quote. Does it support the information in this chapter? Or does it give a different perspective? Explain how in a few sentences.

Many fish are narrow at the front and back. Their smooth sides gradually widen toward the middle.

CHAPTER 3

Body Shape

Many fish's bodies are shaped to move through water with little drag. A streamlined body shape is best for swimming. It is slender at both ends. Curves let water move easily over the body's surface. Easy flow creates less drag.

Blocky Fish

Wide body shapes cause more drag than narrow ones. The ocean sunfish is one of many fish that has an awkward body shape. Its body has flat sides, and its tail is wide and rounded. Like a sail through the air, those shapes interrupt water flow and create drag.

Fish Flying through Air

Flying fish can leap out of the water. They glide through the air for distances of more than 100 feet (30 m) and at speeds of 30 miles per hour (48 km/h). Their fins are broad and long. The fins look like a bird's wings.

Streamlined and Nonstreamlined

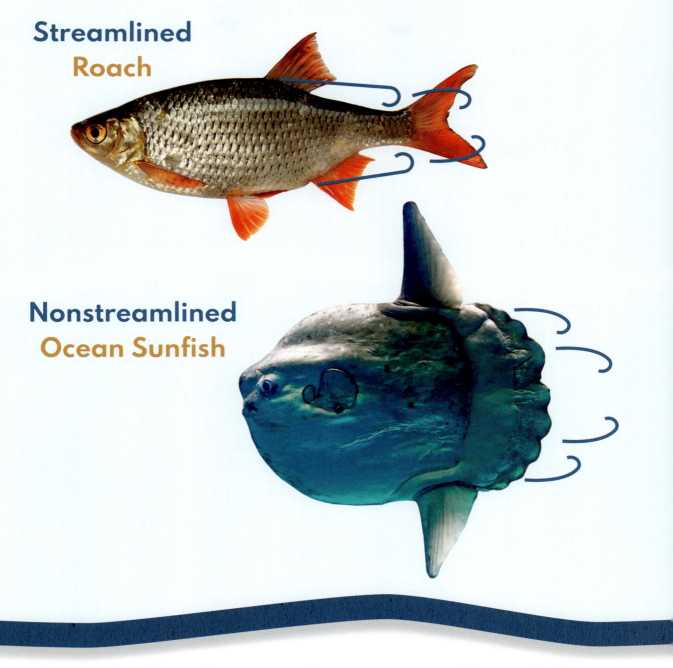

Streamlined
Roach

Nonstreamlined
Ocean Sunfish

This graphic shows how water flows more smoothly over fish with streamlined bodies than fish without streamlined bodies. A streamlined shape helps many fish move quickly in water.

The tail of a billfish is good for swimming fast and far. The tail of a grouper takes more effort to use.

A fish's tail shape tells what kind of swimmer it is. A billfish has a thin, forked tail shaped like a crescent. This tail shape creates strong thrust and little drag. It takes less energy to use, so fish can swim fast for long periods of time. Groupers and other fish with short, rounded tails often start and stop swimming in bursts. They need to rest because their tails create more drag.

Further Evidence

Look at the website below. Does it give any new evidence to support Chapter Three?

How Fish Swim

abdocorelibrary.com/how-fish-swim

Fish can control how deep they are in the water.

CHAPTER 4

Buoyancy

Many fish can adjust their depth without swimming. They do this by changing their buoyancy. Buoyancy is the ability to float. It is caused by a difference in density. Objects that are less dense than the water around them are buoyant.

Great white sharks can swim at the ocean's surface or as deep as nearly 6,200 feet (1,900 m).

Pressure from below pushes up on a buoyant object. At the same time, gravity is a force that pulls objects toward Earth's center. Gravity causes denser objects to sink.

Swim Bladders

Many fish use a swim bladder to control buoyancy. The swim bladder is a small **organ**. It usually holds gas. That gas is typically **oxygen**. Gas is less dense than water.

A fish fills its swim bladder with oxygen from the water. The gas makes the fish's body less dense. The fish rises.

Swimming Up and Down

Fast-swimming fish such as sharks and tuna do not have swim bladders. They change their depth by actively swimming up or down.

A swim bladder helps a fish search for food at different depths.

To sink lower, the fish lets gas out of the bladder. It will keep sinking until it fills its bladder with gas again. To stay at a certain level, the fish fills its swim bladder until the fish is the same density as the water around it.

Each fish has a certain body shape and swimming style to help it survive. But science can explain how all fish swim. Their body shapes and abilities let them move easily through the water.

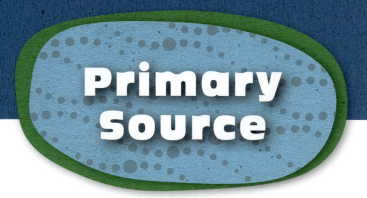

Ocean researcher Betty Staugler explains why fish need buoyancy control:

> [Buoyancy control] allows fish to minimize the energy . . . required to stay at a particular depth to feed, hide, reproduce or **migrate**.

Source: Betty Staugler. "Weightless in the Water." *University of Florida IFAS Blogs*, 25 Oct. 2019, blogs.ifas.ufl.edu. Accessed 27 Sept. 2019.

What's the Big Idea?

What is this quote's main idea? Explain how the main idea is supported by details.

Movement Diagram

Tail and body make multiple curves.

European Conger Eel

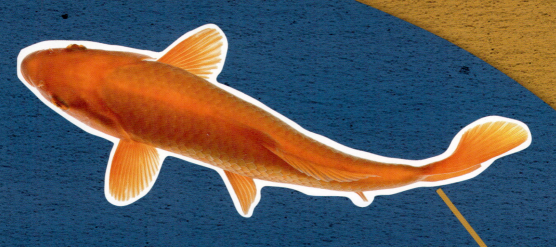

Koi

Tail and body make a single curve.

Movement mainly comes from the tail.

Spotted Boxfish

Glossary

adapt
to change as a species in order to better survive

dorsal fin
an unpaired fin on the back of a fish or whale

horizontal
extending sideways, level with the ground

migrate
to move to another place for a certain period of time

organ
a body part that has a specific purpose

oxygen
a gas that most living things need to survive

particles
tiny pieces of something

Online Resources

To learn more about how fish swim, visit our free resource websites below.

Visit **abdocorelibrary.com** or scan this QR code for free Common Core resources for teachers and students, including vetted activities, multimedia, and booklinks, for deeper subject comprehension.

Visit **abdobooklinks.com** or scan this QR code for free additional online weblinks for further learning. These links are routinely monitored and updated to provide the most current information available.

Learn More

Hansen, Grace. *Becoming a Fish.* Abdo Publishing, 2019.

Kralovansky, Susan. *Whale or Fish?* Abdo Publishing, 2015.

Murray, Julie. *Fish.* Abdo Publishing, 2019.

Index

body fins, 5–6, 9, 14, 18
buoyancy, 23–25, 27

dorsal fins, 12
drag, 11–14, 17–21

flying fish, 18

gravity, 24

Roche, Dominique, 15
resistance, 11, 12

sharks, 12, 25
Staugler, Betty, 27
streamlined body, 17, 19
swim bladders, 25–26

tails, 5–6, 9, 13–14, 18, 21
thrust, 13–14, 21

About the Author

Emma Huddleston lives in the Twin Cities with her husband. She enjoys reading, writing, and swing dancing. She thinks the science of animal movement is fascinating!